I0762648

# AN ANTHOLOGY OF

**WARNING:** This book is an introduction to the amazing world of flowers, and is for general information purposes only. While some flowers are edible, do not eat any plant unless you are very sure of its identification as an edible plant. There are some plants that are poisonous to eat and/or cause severe skin irritations or trigger allergies by touch. If in any doubt, just admire a flower from a distance, and do not touch it.

AN ANTHOLOGY OF

# Flowers

Written by Maddie Bailey
Illustrated by Angela Rizza
and Daniel Long

# Contents

# Types of flower

Flowers come in many shapes, sizes, and colors. Some are cleverly shaped to attract insects and birds to help spread pollen, while others grow in clusters to stand out. From gardens and mountains to deserts, flowers have unique features that help them grow and survive.

## Flower shapes

Flowers bloom in all sorts of delightful shapes—bells, tubes, stars, bowls, and more. Many change their shape and size over time to invite their favorite pollinators. Grouping flowers by shape also helps gardeners know where they grow best and who pollinates them.

## Types of inflorescence

An inflorescence is a cluster of flowers arranged on a plant's stem. It can be of many types. Some, like the simple umbel, grow together to look like fireworks. Others branch out in different ways. When flowers are packed too closely together, it can be harder for pollinators to reach them.

Spadix: Tiny flowers grow on a thick stalk.

Umbel: Several flowers grow from a single point on the stem.

Multiparous cyme: Main stem ends in a flower, with many side branches.

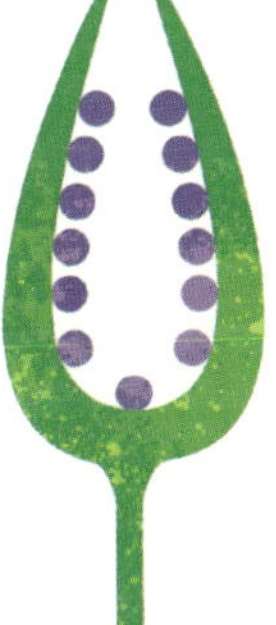

Hypanthodium: Small flowers are grouped inside a hollow structure.

## Flower guide

Flowers can be found in every corner of the world. Some are known by where they grow, such as gardens, rainforests, or mountains. Others are known for their special traits, including fragrance or healing powers. In this book, we look at flowers through these broad themes.

# Life of a plant

In its lifetime, a plant goes through many stages. However, not every plant grows the same way. Some begin as tiny seeds, while others sprout from stems, roots, or leaves. On their growing journey, some plants produce flowers and are called flowering plants, such as blue peas. Others that don't are known as nonflowering plants, such as ferns.

## Different stages

Most flowering plants, like this blue pea, start life as a seed. With the right conditions, including water and sunlight, the hard seed coat softens and splits. A tiny shoot and first roots emerge. The shoot gradually grows leaves, flowers, and fruit. Meanwhile, the roots spread underground, anchoring the plant firmly in the soil.

2

Tiny shoots sprout upward from the seed. Roots grow downward into the soil. This is called germination.

## Lifespan of plants

Plants live for different lengths of time. Some grow quickly and fade away, while others keep blooming, season after season, for many years. Experts group the plants into three types based on how long they live—annual (one year), biennial (two years), and perennial (many years).

# Pollination

Pollination helps flowers make seeds, which then grow new plants. It happens when pollen from the male part of a flower, called the stamen (made up of anther and filament), moves to the female part, called the stigma. Pollinators such as bees, butterflies, birds, and bats carry pollen from flower to flower.

## Parts of a flower

Flowers have special parts that help produce seeds. The anther produces a powdery substance, called pollen, which pollinators carry to other flowers. The stigma is mostly sticky and catches the pollen when pollinators visit. The pollen then grows a tube down to the ovary, where seeds begin to grow.

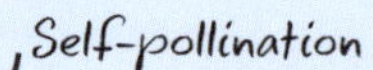

## Types of pollination

Flowers can be pollinated in two ways. Some flowers use their own pollen to form seeds. This is called self-pollination. Others get pollen from different flowers to make seeds because their own pollen can't do the job. This is called cross-pollination.

## Other agents

Along with butterflies, birds, and other animals, wind and water can also help pollinate flowers. Wind blows light pollen through the air, while water carries it across ponds or streams. Wind-pollinated flowers don't need to attract visitors, so they're usually tiny, with no bright colors or strong scents.

## Stages of pollination

Pollination doesn't happen all at once. It takes a little journey. Here is how pollen moves from one flower to another.

1. When flowers are fully grown, they make pollen and nectar.
2. They use sweet smells and bright colors to attract pollinators.
3. A pollinator, like a bee, visits the flower to drink nectar and brushes against the pollen, which sticks to its body.
4. When the bee lands on another flower, some of the pollen rubs off onto its sticky stigma and the flower gets pollinated.
5. The bee flies off and visits more flowers, carrying the pollen with it.

# Garden flowers

You can find gardens all over the world, grown by people who love nature. Gardens are mini habitats. They offer food and shelter to insects, birds, and other animals that live among the trees and plants in parks, backyards, and hanging baskets. Flowers that grow here add vibrant colors, sweet scents, and beauty to everyday life. But they do more than just look pretty or smell nice. They attract visitors, such as bees and butterflies; mark the changing seasons; and remind people of the wonders of nature. Many garden flowers need our care and attention to grow well.

# Sunflower

## *Helianthus annuus*

Sunflowers are a joy to see! But what looks like one big flower is actually made up of lots of tiny flowers. This arrangement is a kind of inflorescence. The bright yellow petals on the outside help insects find the hundreds of small flowers in the middle. When they do, they carry pollen from one bloom to another, helping the middle flowers grow into seeds.

The bouncy yellow petals are known as "ray florets."

*Sunflowers get their name from Helios, the powerful sun god in Greek mythology.*

# Crested cockscomb

## *Celosia argentea var. cristata*

Celosia is a special, sacred flower often planted near temples in India, Myanmar, and China. Commonly known as cockscomb, its bright red flowers look like the comb on a rooster's head. Its young stems and flowers are often cooked in soups and stews.

# Persian buttercup

## *Ranunculus asiaticus*

There are many different types of ranunculus, but this one is grown especially for its beautiful and impressive flowers. Each bloom can stay open for up to 6 weeks. These are called "double flowers" because they have many more petals than usual, giving them a full, lush look.

Ranunculus plants have special roots called tubers, which store food and nutrients.

Layered, ruffled petals form soft folds in these double flowers.

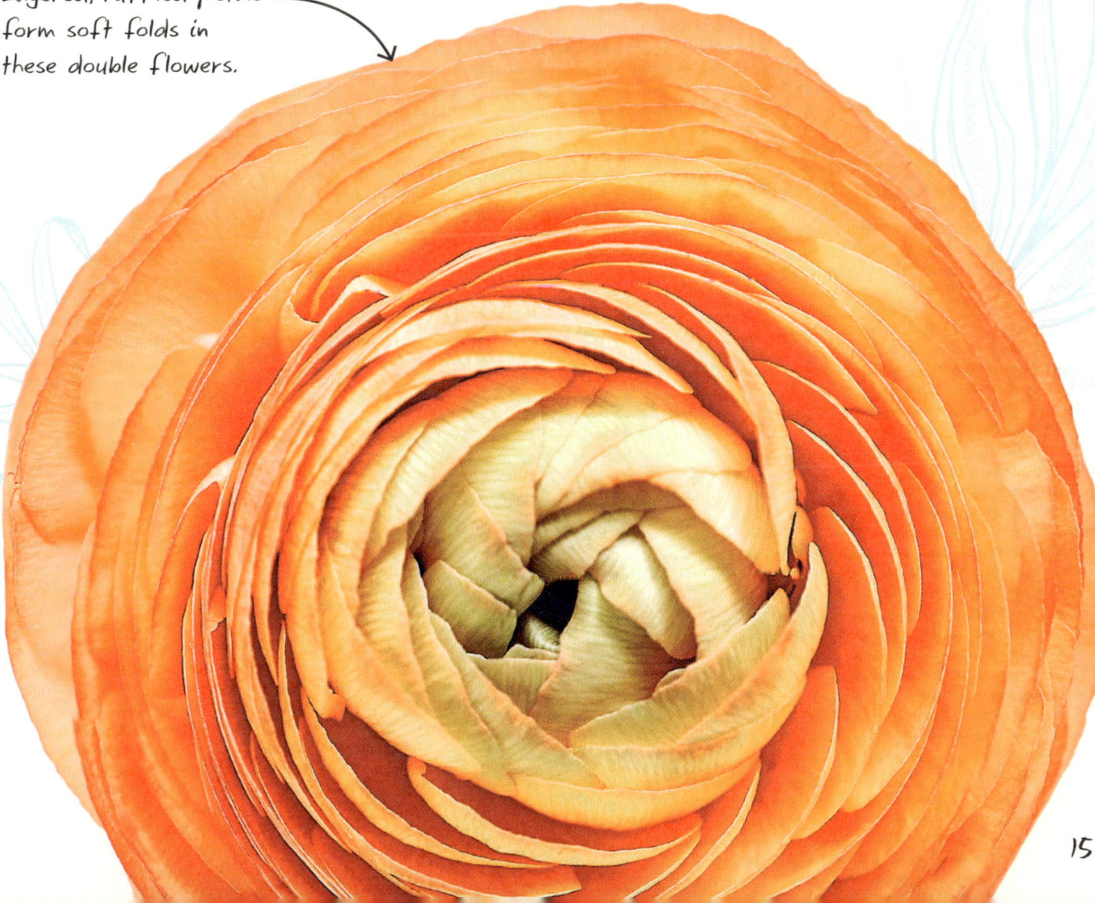

# Tiger lily

## *Lilium lancifolium*

These star-shaped flowers have reddish-orange petals that are covered in dark spots, like the patterns on a tiger's coat. Tiger lilies have sticky, wet pollen that attracts pollinators. Like other lilies, their pollen is harmful to cats.

# Lupin

## *Lupinus polyphyllus*

Lupin belongs to the same plant family as peas and beans, called legumes. Although often grown in gardens, some lupins now grow as invasive wildflowers in Patagonia in South America, New Zealand, and Iceland. Lupin roots can take in nitrogen from the air, turn it into food, and enrich the soil—helping other plants grow.

*Lupin comes from Lupus, meaning "wolf," because it was once believed to "wolf" or steal nutrients from the soil.*

Lupin flowers grow close together on tall spikes

Its blossoms can reach heights of up to 6ft (2m).

Its species name comes from Latin and means "like a bunch of grapes."

# Red hot pokers

## *Kniphofia uvaria*

Red hot pokers come from Africa and are well-adapted to hot, dry conditions. Their tall, spikelike blooms appear in fiery shades of red, orange, and yellow, resembling a flaming torch. Pollinators, such as bees and sunbirds, are frequent visitors to these sun-loving flowers.

# Parrot tulip

## *Tulipa* 'Rasta Parrot'

Parrot tulips are a special hybrid group of tulips. This means they are created by combining two different types of tulip to get their rich, dazzling colors. Many have fringed, feather-like petals that give them the appearance of tropical birds. One of the most striking varieties is the rainbow tulip that flaunts multicolored petals.

# Azalea

## *Rhododendron indicum*

Azaleas brighten gardens with vibrant colors, such as purple, pink, red, white, and blue. They hold special meaning in many countries—especially Japan and China—where springtime azalea festivals are celebrated each year. People from all over the world come to see these beautiful flowers in bloom.

Azalea flowers grow in big clusters.

# Peony

## *Paeonia lactiflora*

There are hundreds of different types of peony, and they are loved all over the world. These sweet-smelling flowers were first grown in Chinese and Japanese gardens more than 3,900 years ago. This species has double flowers—big, fluffy blossoms with a swirl of petals. Many famous artists, such as Édouard Manet, painted peonies in their work.

# Bougainvillea

## *Bougainvillea spectabilis*

Bougainvillea flowers grow on thorny vines in warm regions of the world. Their tiny flowers typically bloom in groups of three, surrounded by brightly colored leaves that pretend to be petals. These leaves are called bracts and help attract pollinators with their brilliant shades of pink, purple, orange, or white.

# Dahlia

## *Dahlia pinnata*

Dahlias have 2 to 8 small flowers called florets that make up the big, showy flower. These blooms are grown around the world, but originate from Mexico, where they are also the national flower. The world's largest flower parade, held in the Netherlands each September, showcases only dahlias—around eight million of them!

Each floret has oval-shaped petals.

# Hydrangea

## *Hydrangea macrophylla*

Hydrangeas produce large flower clusters that stand out like giant pompoms in a garden. They have a special ability to change color based on the soil. In acidic soil, the flowers turn blue. In alkaline soil, they become pink. If the soil is somewhere in between, the hydrangeas bloom purple—a mix of pink and blue.

Their flower heads can be round, flat-topped, or cone-shaped.

Distinct veins help transport water and nutrients.

# Strawflower

## *Xerochrysum bracteatum*

Commonly called "golden everlasting flowers," strawflowers get their name from the stiff, crispy petals that look like straw. These unique petals can dry easily and do not wilt or die. Native to Australia, strawflowers grow happily in gardens, but can also be found in deserts, in rainforests, and on mountains.

In gardens, their bracts are normally pink, red, or white.

Strawflowers belong to the aster family, just like daisies, dahlias, and sunflowers.

# Colors explained

Flowers use colors like a superpower. Some flaunt a single bold shade, while others display a mix of vibrant colors. Their bright petals stand out against the green leaves, making it easy for pollinators to spot them. For bees, butterflies, and other visitors, color is the first hint that something sweet is nearby.

*Anthocyanins create purple, pink, blue, and even black.*

## Pretty pigments

Flowers get their colors from pigments like anthocyanins and carotenoids. These pigments produce reds, blues, yellows, or mixed colors. But color isn't just about pigments—light, temperature, soil, and even drought or poor nutrition can all affect how a flower looks.

Flowers with anthocyanins

*Carotenoids make bright oranges, yellows, and reds.*

Flowers with carotenoids

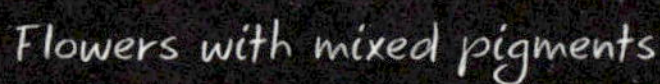

Flowers with mixed pigments

## Spotting colors

Different insects are better at seeing certain colors of light. Bees are best at spotting yellow, blue, and green. Butterflies are drawn to warm shades, such as red, pink, and orange. Nighttime visitors like bats and moths have poor eyesight, so they prefer big white flowers that are easy to spot in the dark.

*Most flowers have special patterns that can only be seen under UV light.*

## Insect vision

Insects see differently from us. Their vision is blurry, but they can spot colors and ultraviolet (UV) light that we can't. Flowers often glow and reveal hidden patterns under UV light. Some even change petal colors to help their insect friends find them more easily.

*This is how a sunflower appears to humans under normal light.*

*This is how the insects see the same flower.*

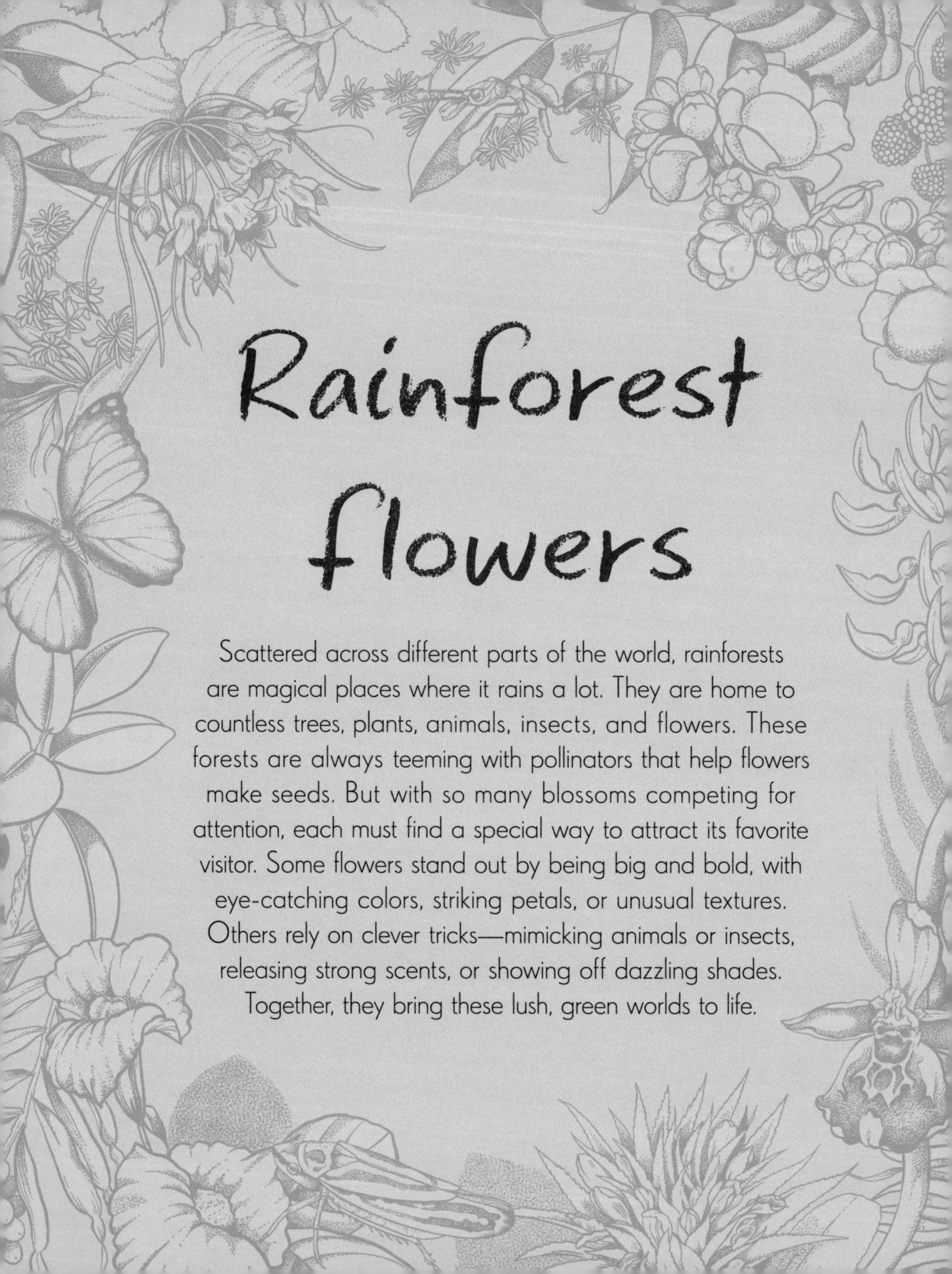

# Rainforest flowers

Scattered across different parts of the world, rainforests are magical places where it rains a lot. They are home to countless trees, plants, animals, insects, and flowers. These forests are always teeming with pollinators that help flowers make seeds. But with so many blossoms competing for attention, each must find a special way to attract its favorite visitor. Some flowers stand out by being big and bold, with eye-catching colors, striking petals, or unusual textures. Others rely on clever tricks—mimicking animals or insects, releasing strong scents, or showing off dazzling shades. Together, they bring these lush, green worlds to life.

# Passionflower

## *Passiflora caerulea*

With brightly colored petals, frizzy filaments, and delicious fruit, passionflowers look as if they belong in a fantasy world! There are hundreds of species and each one looks different. Scientists think this is because the flowers attract a wide variety of pollinators, including bees, butterflies, and hummingbirds.

The tubular flowers cleverly hide inside the bracts.

# Hanging lobster claw

## *Heliconia rostrata*

Also called false birds of paradise, these plants grow deep in the tropical rainforests of Central America. Their tiny flowers pop out of big, lobster-claw-shaped bracts, hence the name. The bracts hold water for birds that stop to drink, and in return they pollinate the flowers.

# Bee orchid

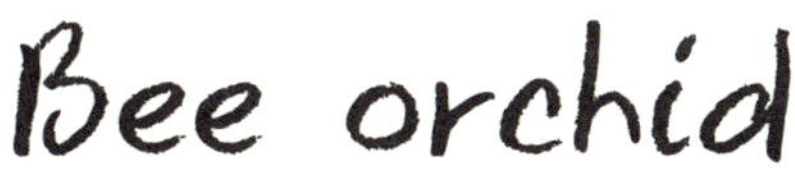

## *Ophrys bombyliflora*

These orchids are master tricksters. They mimic female bumblebees—looking and smelling like them—to attract male bees for pollination. They look so similar that sometimes the male bees try to impress the flower instead of a real female bee!

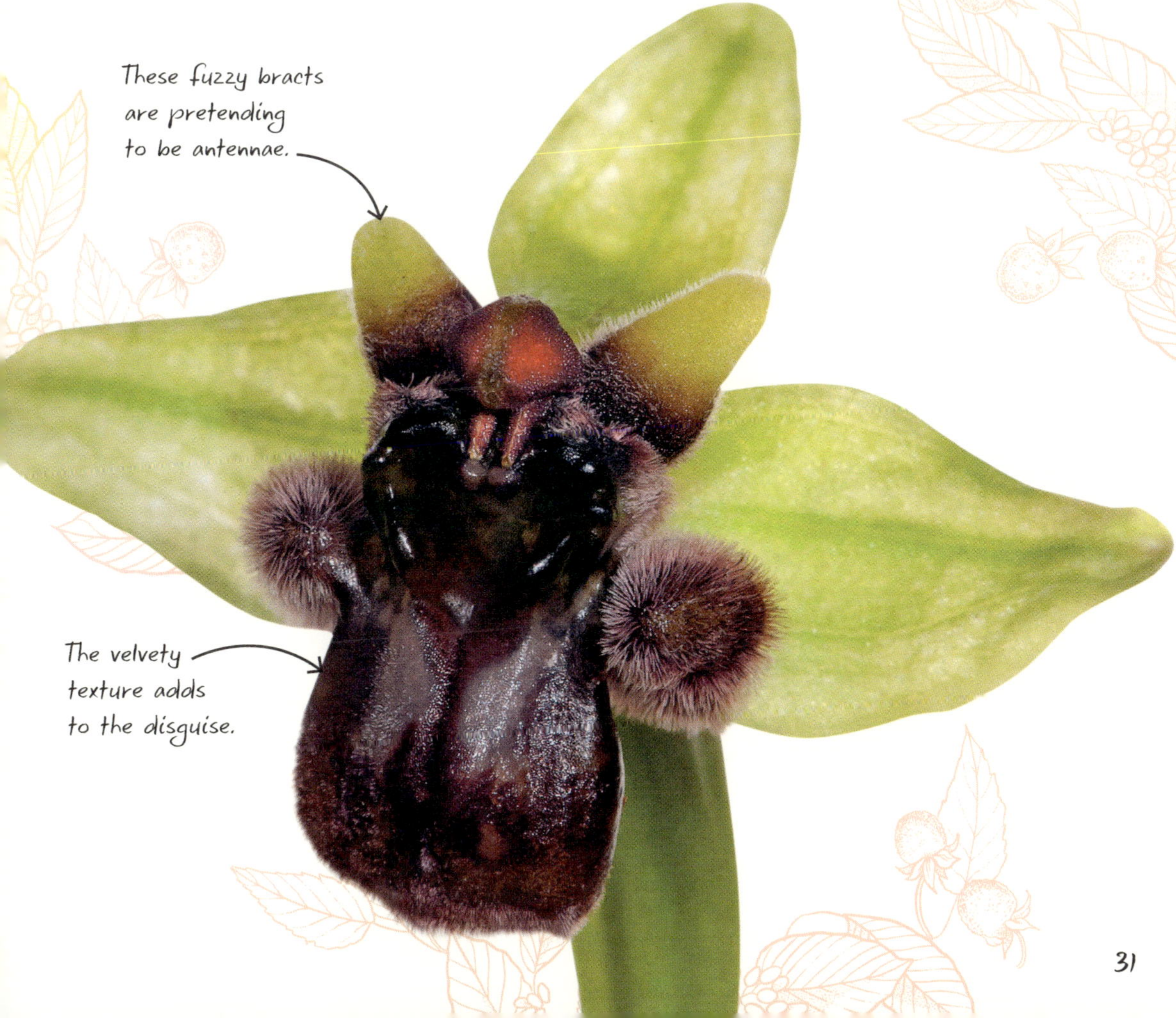
These fuzzy bracts are pretending to be antennae.
The velvety texture adds to the disguise.

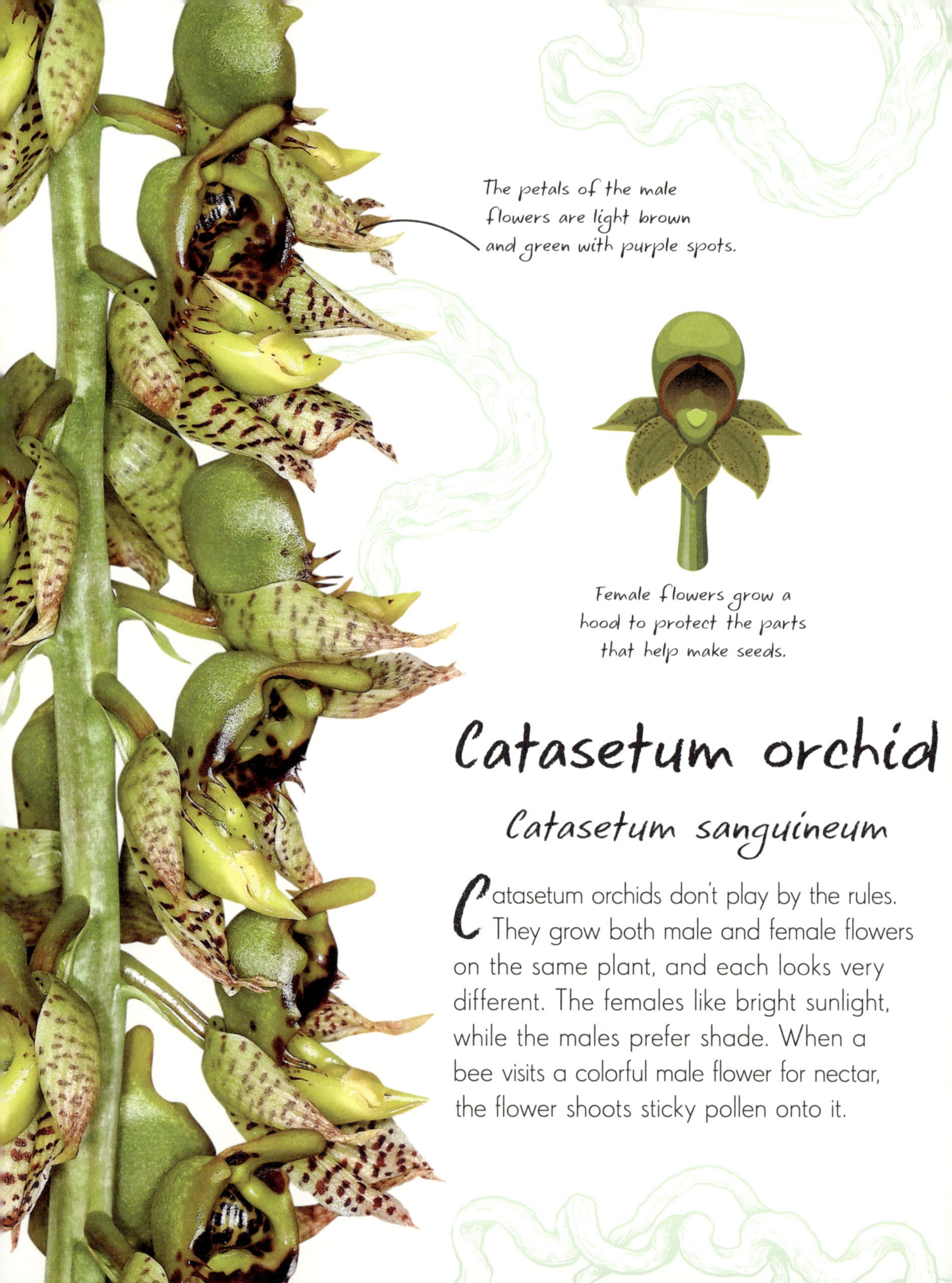


# Catasetum orchid

## *Catasetum sanguineum*

Catasetum orchids don't play by the rules. They grow both male and female flowers on the same plant, and each looks very different. The females like bright sunlight, while the males prefer shade. When a bee visits a colorful male flower for nectar, the flower shoots sticky pollen onto it.

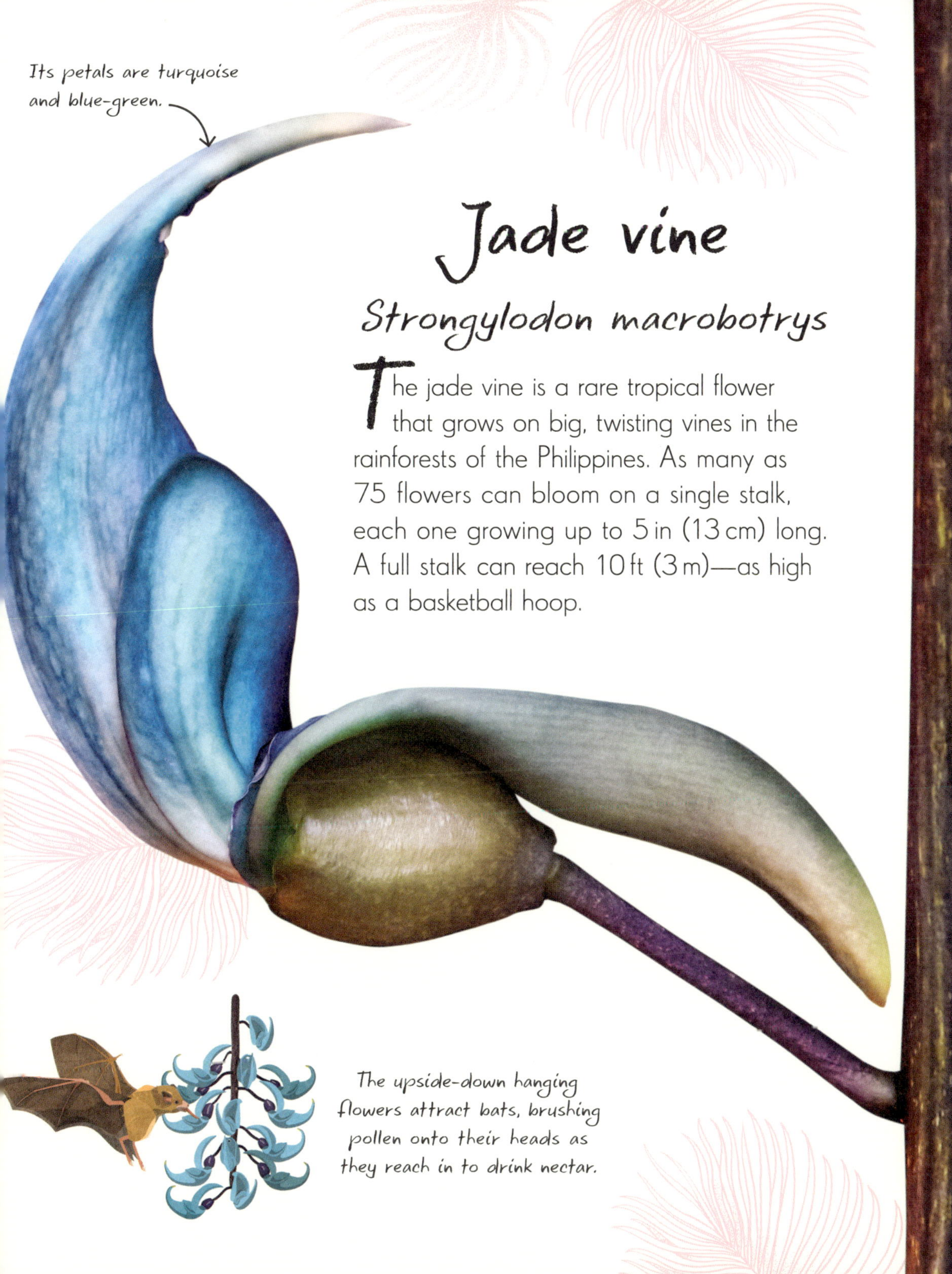


# Jade vine

## *Strongylodon macrobotrys*

The jade vine is a rare tropical flower that grows on big, twisting vines in the rainforests of the Philippines. As many as 75 flowers can bloom on a single stalk, each one growing up to 5 in (13 cm) long. A full stalk can reach 10 ft (3 m)—as high as a basketball hoop.

# Black bat flower

## *Tacca chantrieri*

This is one of the strangest-looking flowers in the world. It has dark, winglike bracts and long, hairy whiskers that can dangle up to 10 in (25 cm). Found across Asia, this flower doesn't just look like a bat, but also thrives in the shade like the animal it's named after. It can also pollinate itself, without any help from insects or other pollinators.

Tiny clusters of flowers grow within the bracts.

# Urn plant

## *Aechmea fasciata*

Urn plants are native to Brazil and belong to the same family as pineapples. Their flowering head is made of brightly colored bracts that attract pollinators—especially their favorites, the hummingbirds. Between the bracts grow lots of small purple flowers that look like shining gemstones.

The bracts have spiky edges, like teeth.

# Hot lips

## *Palicourea elata*

This flower looks just like a pair of big red lips ready for a kiss! But the "lips" are actually bracts— special leaves that protect the real flower. When it is time, tiny flowers pop out from between the lips. They don't smell strong, but the bright bracts attract a host of birds, butterflies, and moths.

In Central America, people see hot lips as a symbol of love.

The flower is shaped like a tiny star.

# Queen of the night

## *Epiphyllum oxypetalum*

Queen of the night is one of the most special flowers of the rainforest. Its delicate, scented blossoms last for just one night—opening at dusk and wilting at the break of dawn. Anyone who sees them in full bloom is truly lucky.

The cold temperature helps the soft petals open up at night.

Its pale flowers can grow as big as dinner plates, allowing bats to spot and pollinate them in the dark.

# Mountain flowers

High on mountaintops, the air is thin and cold, with no protection from the harsh sun or drying winds. The flowers that grow here are tough and resilient. Many have thick hairs on their stems and leaves to guard against intense sunlight, freezing temperatures, and frost. The flowers also grow close to the ground to avoid being blown away. While most flowers rely on the wind for pollination, insects such as bumblebees lend a helping hand on sunny days. Lower down, near trees and streams, flowers find more shelter and animal visitors. There, they grow taller, with bigger flowers and more leaves.

# Himalayan blue poppy

## *Meconopsis betonicifolia*

Tucked high in the Himalayan mountains of Asia, this striking flower is known for its rare, vivid blue color. Ranging from pale sky blue to deep violet, the unique color comes from the special mix of soil and sunlight where it grows. Himalayan poppies are the national flower of Bhutan, where they represent happiness and peace.

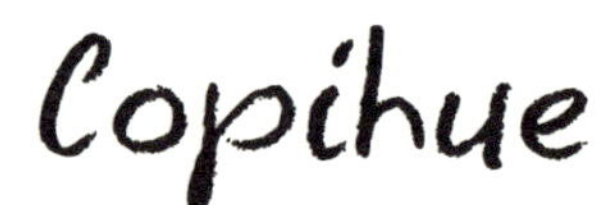

# Copihue

## *Lapageria rosea*

Copihue flowers grow only in the mountains of Chile. With their bright, bell-shaped blooms, it is easy to see why they're also called the Chilean bellflower. This special blossom is Chile's national flower, and picking it is illegal—something that has helped keep this beauty from disappearing from the wild.

Thick and strong petals help it cope with the bitter cold.

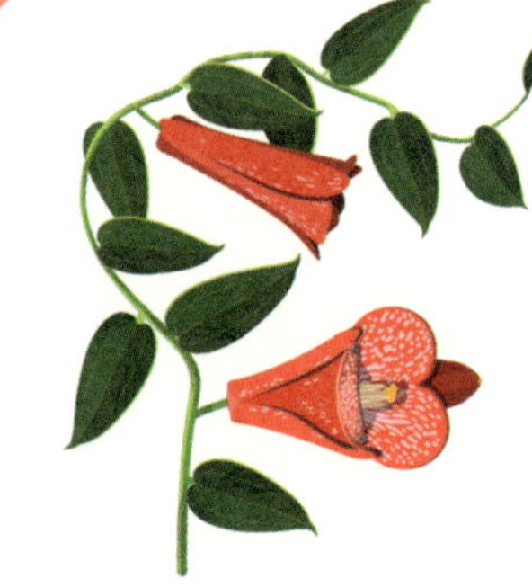

It can take 10 years for a copihue to make its first flowers.

The soft, white flowers are shaped like stars.

# Edelweiss

## *Leontopodium nivale*

Edelweiss is a treasured flower in the alpine regions of Europe. It is admired not just for its beauty but also for symbolizing purity and courage. The small flowers are surrounded by white petals covered in silvery hairs that look like cotton. This protects them from the blazing sun and biting cold.

# Yellow avalanche lily

## *Erythronium grandiflorum*

Yellow avalanche lilies grow in the mountains of North America, where they are a favorite food of grizzly and black bears. These bright flowers pop up in spring, just after the snow melts, turning mountains and valleys yellow. Their vivid color attracts their favorite pollinators—bumblebees!

# Porcelain orchid

## *Chloraea magellanica*

Porcelain orchids are among the toughest orchids in the world. They grow in the mountains of southern Argentina and Chile, where winters are harsh. These hardy plants can stay buried under snow for up to 8 months and survive temperatures as low as -4°F (-20°C). Their flowers bloom in spring, once the snow has melted.

*The porcelain orchid is the first colorless orchid species discovered in Chile.*

Its white petals are marked with bright green netlike patterns.

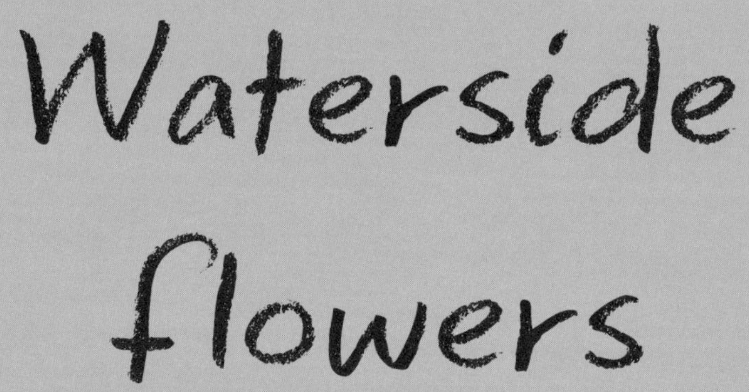

# Waterside flowers

Waterside flowers bloom along the edges of ponds, rivers, lakes, swamps, and seas. Some grow with their roots deep in the water, while others stay close to the shore on firmer ground. Living near water takes special skills and these flowers are well adapted. Bees, butterflies, and dragonflies help them share pollen without it getting soaked. Some flowers use the wind and a few even let the water carry their pollen. These flowers aren't just beautiful to look at, they play an important role. They help keep the soil from washing away; add oxygen to the water; and provide food for fish, birds, and bugs.

# Lotus

## *Nelumbo nucifera*

Lotus is a symbol of beauty and purity across southern Asia. As India's national flower, it is offered to Hindu gods and goddesses during prayers. These stunning flowers rise above the water, while their broad leaves float gently on the surface and the roots dig deep into the muddy bottom.

Once the flower is pollinated, petals fall off and a seed pod grows from a small green bud.

Lotuses come in shades of pink, white, and yellow.

They are named after the bright red robes worn by cardinals, who are senior priests in the Catholic Church.

# Cardinal flower

## *Lobelia cardinalis*

Cardinal flowers make their homes in the bogs and swamps of the Americas, surrounded by trees, reptiles, and birds. Their bright red flowers bloom from early spring until the end of fall, and are a favorite stop for tiny ruby-throated hummingbirds.

# Cattail

## *Typha latifolia*

Cattails, also known as bulrushes, bloom along the edges of ponds, lakes, and marshes. You'll often find them keeping company with frogs, ducks, and dragonflies. Their flowers grow on tall spikes and look like giant brown sausages. Some of the flowers can be as long as 12 in (30 cm).

Small, dangly male flowers

The sausage-like part is made up of female flowers.

The plant's long, flat leaves are used to make mats and chair seats.

# Papyrus

## *Cyperus papyrus*

Papyrus grows in wetlands across Africa, especially along the Nile River in Egypt. Ancient Egyptians used it to make many things, such as boats, baskets, and sandals. Its stalks were used to create one of the world's first forms of paper, also called papyrus.

# Wavy marshwort

## *Nymphoides crenata*

Wavy marshwort is found in Australian swamps that flood easily during wet weather. Its tightly packed underwater leaves help keep it afloat. Although its flowers are only 1 in (3 cm) wide, the bright yellow color can light up even the murkiest of swamps.

# Desert flowers

Deserts are dry, sunny places where water is scarce and life isn't easy. They can be scorching hot during the day, but freezing cold at night. Despite these extreme conditions, many reptiles, birds, insects, plants, and flowers live here. Because there aren't always many pollinators around, desert flowers have several ways to get noticed. Some put on a colorful show to stand out against the sand. Others release strong scents or open their petals only at night to draw the attention of nighttime visitors like moths. These clever hacks help desert flowers thrive in one of the toughest places on Earth.

# Fairy duster

## *Calliandra eriophylla*

Fairy duster flowers brighten the deserts in North America. Their fluffy pompoms attract all kinds of guests, such as bees, flies, butterflies, and hummingbirds. These sweet hosts also offer plenty of nectar to keep their pollinator friends coming back for more.

# Desert globe mallow

## *Sphaeralcea ambigua*

Desert globe mallows love hot places, such as Arizona, Nevada, and New Mexico in North America. They bloom most of the year and attract bees, butterflies, moths, and hummingbirds. These sun-loving flowers also provide shelter to endangered desert tortoises, who love snacking on their leaves!

Some people call them "eye-sore poppies" because their fuzzy leaves can cause itchiness if they touch your eyes.

Apricot-colored flowers

The petals are dotted with dark red speckles.

# Ghost flower

## *Mohavea confertiflora*

Ghost flowers aren't called that because they're spooky. The name comes from their pale, almost see-through petals that give them a ghostly look. Since they don't make any nectar of their own, the pale blooms mimic other nectar-rich flowers to trick bees into visiting.

# Kangaroo paw

## *Anigozanthos manglesii*

It's easy to see how this flower got its name—when the bloom opens, it looks just like a kangaroo's paw. These quirky flowers thrive in Australia's hot, dry landscapes and come in shades of red, orange, black, and yellow. While sipping nectar, birds pick up pollen on their heads and pass it along to other flowers.

# Sugarbush

## *Protea repens*

Sugarbush flowers are an inflorescence—a bunch of tiny flowers packed together in the center, surrounded by bright outer bracts. Native to South Africa, they produce plenty of nectar to draw in birds, insects, and other desert animals.

The name *Protea* comes from the shape-shifting Greek god Proteus, as the flowers grow in many different shapes.

The bracts can be pink, cream, or red.

This prominent black circle is called the "boss" of the flower.

# Sturt's desert pea

## Sp. Swainsona formosa

Desert peas get their name from their close relation to the legume family. They flourish in the heart of Australia, far from the sea, along creek beds and on stony hills. Their bright red petals appear in clusters at the top of stems and are often visited by insects and birds alike.

The desert pea usually grows in clusters of 5 to 6 flowers.

# Bird-of-paradise flower

## *Strelitzia reginae*

It's easy to see why this flower is called the bird-of-paradise—its flowering head resembles a tropical bird. There are only five types in the world. Three have white flowers, while the other two display bright blue and orange blooms. In South Africa, its seeds are traditionally used to sour milk.

# Jackal food

## Hydnora africana

In the deserts of Africa, jackal food flowers release a strong, stinky smell to attract carrion beetles and dung beetles. When a beetle arrives, the flower snaps shut to trap it, making sure it picks up lots of pollen. A few days later, the flower opens again and the insect flies off to pollinate the next flower.

Its vibrant green flowers are only 1.6 in (2 cm) long.

# Green bird flower

## *Crotalaria cunninghamii*

Found in Australia's hot deserts, these flowers mimic tiny green hummingbirds pecking at plant stems. It's unclear if their shape attracts pollinators or warns off animals that might eat them. Their scientific name comes from the Greek word for "rattle." When the flowers fade, the seeds make a rattling sound inside their pods.

The flowers hang out in clusters on the tips of the stems.

# Wildflowers

Wildflowers are nature's little adventurers. They grow all by themselves with no help from people. You can see them popping up in all kinds of places, such as forests, grasslands, mountains, and hills. Those that are native to the countries and regions where they grow are super important because they feed bees, butterflies, and all sorts of insects. Without these wild beauties, life would be much harder for the creatures around them. Spotting them in nature brings joy to those who behold them, while adding a dash of color and magic to the wild.

# Billy button

## *Pycnosorus globosus*

Native to Australia and New Zealand, billy buttons are like little yellow bouncy balls. Each flower head holds up to 200 tiny "pretend" flowers, and inside each one are about eight mini flowers. They're like a flower version of a Russian nesting doll, with surprise after surprise tucked inside.

*Bees love billy buttons the most, but they're also visited by moths at night.*

The flowers look like buttons on a jacket or cardigan.

# Dandelion

## *Taraxacum officinale*

Dandelions have been around for several centuries and are loved by pollinators, especially bees. Early-spring insects rely on them for food when other flowers haven't woken up yet. Once pollinated, the dandelion flowers turn into a seed head full of tiny seeds attached to parachutes that fly away in the wind.

The yellow dandelion flowers growing in the wild are often called "little suns in the grass."

# Poppy

## *Papaver rhoeas*

Symbols of love and remembrance, poppies are a sight to behold in wild meadows. The wind scatters their seeds, and ample sunlight and water help these beauties to bloom. When they are ready to flower, the sepals curl back, unfurling the petals in vibrant shades of red.

# Daisy

## *Bellis perennis*

Daisies brighten lawns, riverbanks, and grassy hillsides all across Europe and Australia. Their yellow faces turn toward the sun, just like sunflowers, and shut at night. The bright yellow center isn't just one flower, but a cluster of tiny flowers called disk florets. Full of charm, daisies are adored by many and often represent innocence and purity in different cultures.

Ladybugs love to stop by daisies.

Their pale pink or white flowers are shaped like a trumpet.

# Hedge bindweed

## *Convolvulus arvensis*

Twisted vines of hedge bindweed grow very swiftly. They often show up uninvited in gardens, which is why many people call them weeds. In fact, they are essential to the environment, because they provide food to more than 80 different species of insects in wildflower meadows.

# Wild angelica

## Angelica sylvestris

Their reddish-brown seeds are used as a spice in many countries.

The tiny umbrellas of wild angelica love wet, shady spots, such as marshes, woodlands, and wetland meadows. These delicate flowers are a treat for a host of insects, including bees, beetles, and hoverflies. Wherever these blooms grow, be sure the soil is rich and healthy.

Angelica flowers look like dreamy fireworks!

# Bluebell

## *Hyacinthoides non-scripta*

In spring, woodlands across Europe turn into majestic carpets of blooming bluebells. These popular flowers are believed to grow mostly in woodlands that are at least 500 years old. The fruity bluebells burst with nectar and have cream-colored pollen, which are a pollinator's delight.

# Wild daffodil

## *Narcissus pseudonarcissus*

Every spring, wild daffodils bloom across Western Europe, turning woodlands and grasslands into seas of yellow. The flowers get a little help from ants, who carry their seeds to nibble on the tasty outer coating. When they're done, they toss the leftover seed into a quiet corner, where a new daffodil grows.

The bright reddish-purple color fuchsia is named after the colors of the chilco flowers.

# Chilco

## *Fuchsia magellanica*

The dangling chilco flowers come in captivating hues of red, purple, and pink. Their pollinator friends like hummingbirds lose their heart to the red petals. They naturally grow in large numbers in Argentina and Chile, but garden lovers around the world have started growing them, too.

In Victorian times, the drooping chilco flower was called "lady's eardrops."

# Cotton thistle

## *Onopordum acanthium*

The cotton thistle is often mistaken for the Scottish thistle for their similar appearance. While both are prickly, cotton thistle leaves have cotton-like hairs. They are a special treat for bees, butterflies, flies, and moths, who visit them to sip sweet nectar. Cotton thistles are commonly found in Europe and Asia.

Since this plant is covered with spikes, animals find it hard to munch on it.

Their flower heads have countless purple petals.

# Diego de la noche

## *Mirabilis jalapa*

Diego de la noche, also called the four o'clock flower, has a magical bedtime routine. The flowers open up after 4 p.m. and fill the air with a sweet smell all night long. That's how it calls in its favorite nighttime visitors—moths. Before sunrise, the flowers gently close up again, ready to rest until the next evening.

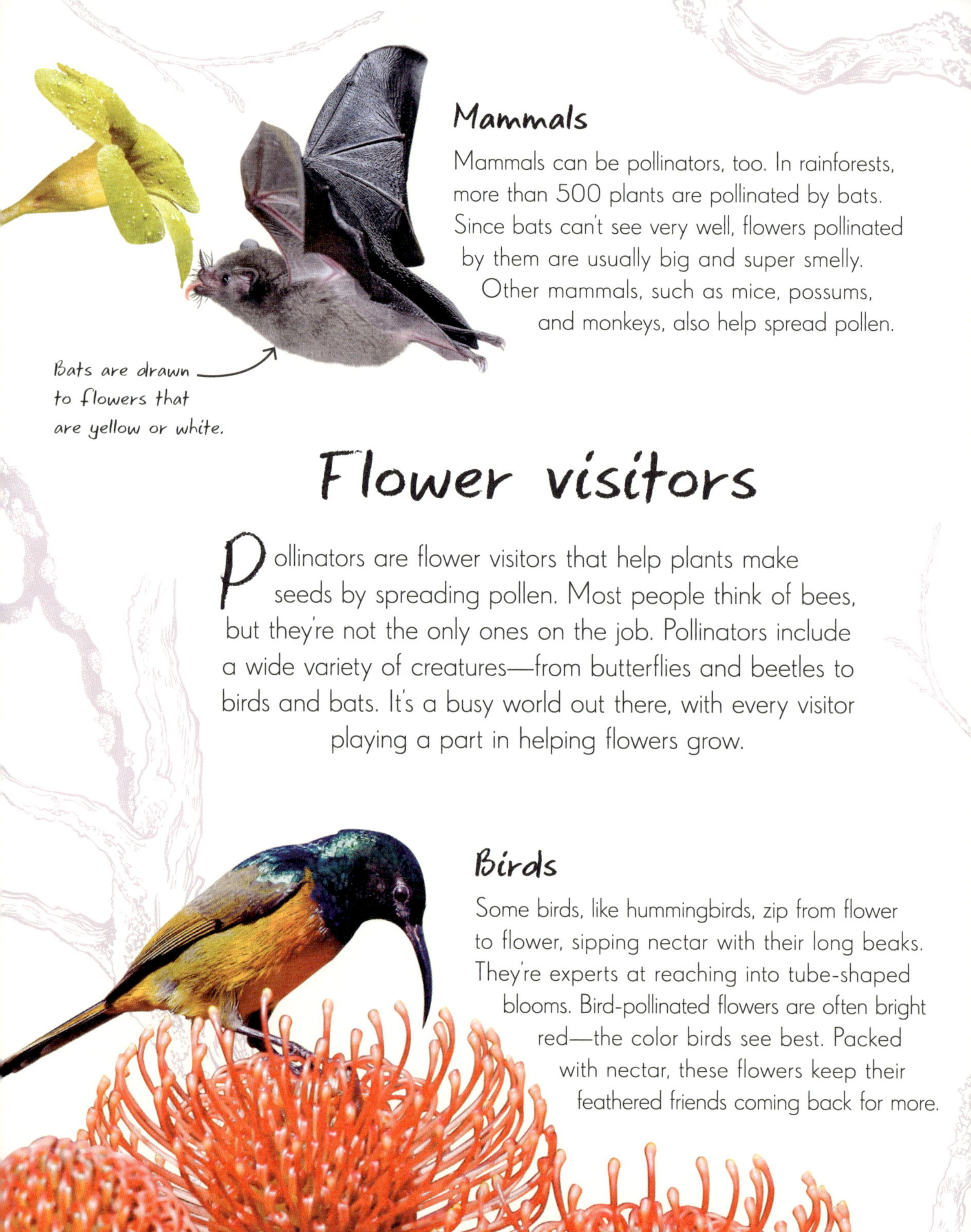

## Mammals

Mammals can be pollinators, too. In rainforests, more than 500 plants are pollinated by bats. Since bats can't see very well, flowers pollinated by them are usually big and super smelly. Other mammals, such as mice, possums, and monkeys, also help spread pollen.

Bats are drawn to flowers that are yellow or white.

# Flower visitors

Pollinators are flower visitors that help plants make seeds by spreading pollen. Most people think of bees, but they're not the only ones on the job. Pollinators include a wide variety of creatures—from butterflies and beetles to birds and bats. It's a busy world out there, with every visitor playing a part in helping flowers grow.

## Birds

Some birds, like hummingbirds, zip from flower to flower, sipping nectar with their long beaks. They're experts at reaching into tube-shaped blooms. Bird-pollinated flowers are often bright red—the color birds see best. Packed with nectar, these flowers keep their feathered friends coming back for more.

*Butterflies are attracted to pink, red, orange, and purple flowers.*

## Trickster flowers

Some flowers are clever tricksters. They pretend to be birds, insects, or animals by making patterns on their petals or producing smells. This can fool pollinators into thinking they've found a friend, partner, or an enemy.

## Insects

Insect pollinators are the busiest and most common. Bees, wasps, flies, butterflies, beetles, and moths all help carry pollen from flower to flower. Because there are so many different types of insect, the flowers they visit come in many shapes, sizes, and colors to suit their tiny visitors.

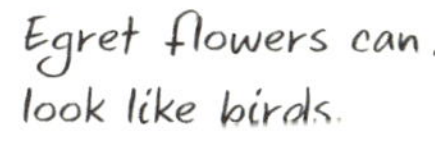

*Egret flowers can look like birds.*

## Unexpected helpers

Field mice sometimes help flowers without even knowing it. When they visit flowers to snack on pollen, some of it sticks to their noses. Then, as they move to other flowers, they accidentally spread the pollen around. Some flowers make more pollen when mice are most active, hoping to tempt them back for another visit.

Not all flowers play nicely! Some wildflowers can be harmful or even poisonous. While they may look beautiful, these blooms contain strong chemicals that can make animals and people sick if touched or eaten. Just like plants with thorns or stinging hairs, these natural defenses help protect the flowers from being gobbled up before they can grow seeds. Many wild plants use special tactics to protect themselves, but not all of them are harmful. However, it is best to admire flowers from a safe distance—some may seem harmless but hide a deadly secret.

# Foxglove

## *Digitalis purpurea*

Foxglove flowers bloom gracefully on a tall, slender spike. Though poisonous if eaten, they have been used by doctors to treat heart problems for hundreds of years. In some folk tales, mischievous foxes wore foxglove flowers on their feet to sneak up on chickens unnoticed.

# Hemlock

## *Conium maculatum*

Hemlock is the fatal cousin of wild angelica and carrots. While all parts of this plant are poisonous, the seeds of hemlock have the most amount of toxin. Native to Europe, western Asia, and North America, the white hemlock flowers elegantly grow in an umbrella shape along rivers and streams.

# Wolfsbane

## *Aconitum napellus*

The flowers of wolfsbane may please your eyes, but beware—they can be dangerous! Even a simple touch can sometimes be harmful. Legends tell that they could scare off werewolves. The ancient Greeks also used them to hunt wild animals. Despite the poison, wolfsbane is often grown in gardens for its striking purple or white flowers.

Wolfsbane flowers grow on tall slender spikes, branching from both sides.

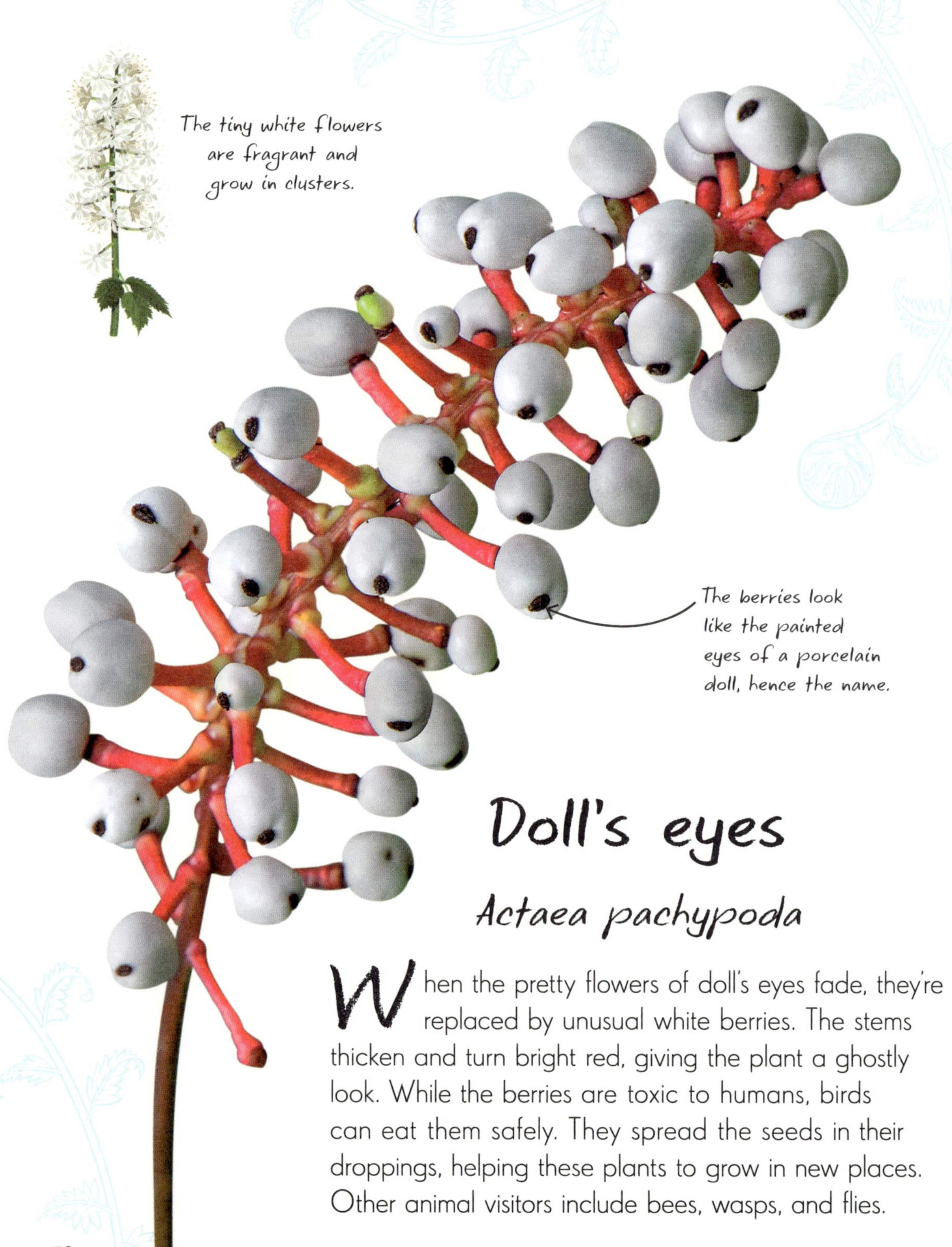


# Doll's eyes

## *Actaea pachypoda*

When the pretty flowers of doll's eyes fade, they're replaced by unusual white berries. The stems thicken and turn bright red, giving the plant a ghostly look. While the berries are toxic to humans, birds can eat them safely. They spread the seeds in their droppings, helping these plants to grow in new places. Other animal visitors include bees, wasps, and flies.

# Angel's trumpet

## *Brugmansia suaveolens*

Related to potatoes, angel's trumpets get their name from their trumpet-shaped flowers. These delicate blossoms hang from trees and release a sweet scent at night to attract nighttime pollinators. If a person eats one, it can cause hallucinations—making them see and hear things that aren't really happening. The flowers are usually white but also come in shades of yellow and pink.

# Deadly nightshade

## *Atropa bella-donna*

This is one of the most poisonous plants known to humans. Long ago, it was believed to be a witch's favorite—used as a key ingredient in potions. Its glossy berries may seem appealing, but the plant contains a toxin named atropine, which can cause hallucinations. The plant is so poisonous that even the bees that drink its nectar produce toxic honey.

*When the flowers wilt, they're replaced by black, shiny berries.*

*The bell-shaped flowers usually have five petals, which are joined together.*

This species has white flowers, unlike its pink-flowered, similarly scented cousin.

*In France, May 1 is celebrated as Lily of the Valley Day, when people gift these flowers for good luck.*

# Lily of the valley

## *Convallaria majalis*

Prized for its rich scent, lily of the valley blooms in spring. It can produce up to 15 bell-shaped flowers on a single stem at once. This low-growing plant thrives in shady woodlands across Europe and Asia. Although pretty to look at, the plant contains chemicals that can be highly toxic to humans and pets.

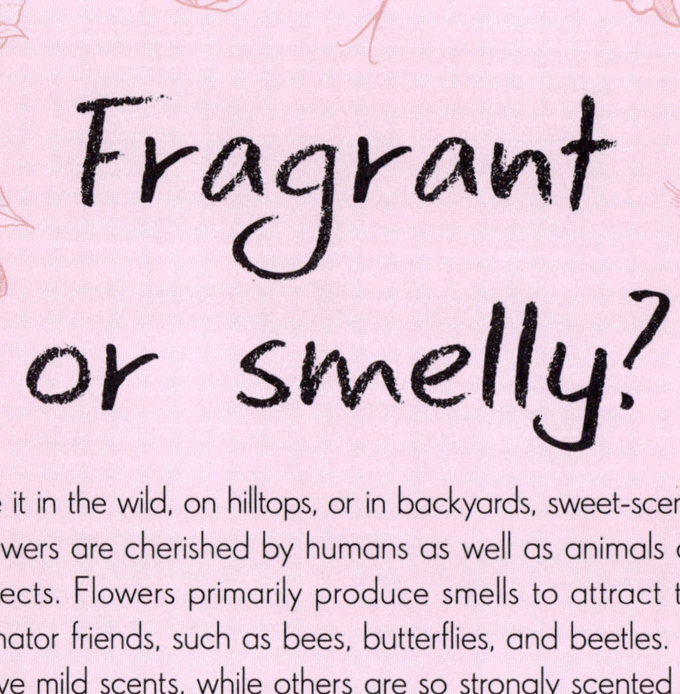

# Fragrant or smelly?

Be it in the wild, on hilltops, or in backyards, sweet-scented flowers are cherished by humans as well as animals and insects. Flowers primarily produce smells to attract their pollinator friends, such as bees, butterflies, and beetles. Some have mild scents, while others are so strongly scented that they can be detected from far away. For centuries, people have been using floral scents to make perfumes, essential oils, and soaps. But not all flowers are a treat for the nose. Some wild ones smell awful, like rotting meat, fish, smelly feet, or even poop. These stinky flowers help plants trick insects, such as beetles and flies, into pollinating them.

# Sweet pea

## *Lathyrus odoratus*

Fluttering in the summer breeze, sweet pea is a sight to behold! Its blooms burst in shades of pink, purple, blue, or white. Just like its legume cousins, it also has slender stems called tendrils. They twist around nearby plants for support and climb upward, following the sunlight. Sweet pea flowers have a fruity fragrance, as suggested by the Latin name *odoratus*, meaning "sweet smelling."

The fruit of some rose plants, called rose hips, are widely used in medicines.

While yellow roses stand for friendship, apricot roses like this one symbolize gratitude.

# Rose

## *Rosa sp.*

Roses are one of the most loved flowers in the world. With colors, such as yellow, red, pink, and white, they brighten up gardens everywhere. Some roses have a pleasant smell and are widely used in perfumes, lotions, and soaps. Others have no scent at all.

# Snowdrop

## *Galanthus nivalis*

Sweet smelling snowdrops are a winter delight. These little flowers push up through deep snow on sturdy green stems. Their droopy white heads often have special markings, depending on the species. Snowdrops are cherished by many and used in several scented products.

# Frangipani

## *Plumeria rubra*

Frangipani is known across Southeast and East Asia for its sweet tropical scent. Its fragrance is used in incense, oils, and perfumes. However, most parts of the plant are poisonous. Its milk sap can irritate the skin, and eating other parts may cause vomiting.

*Frangipani releases its sweet scent at night to attract nighttime pollinators, especially the sphinx moth.*

Its flowers can be pink, red, or white, often with yellow in the center.

# Jasmine

## *Jasminum officinale*

The delightful scent of jasmine can often be recognized with just one sniff. Its fragrance is the strongest in the evening, just when moths wake up and come to visit. A village in Egypt, called Shubra Beloula, produces over half the world's jasmine for perfumes. Many people also enjoy its delicate flavor in tea.

# Stapelia

## Stapelia grandiflora

Stapelia, or starfish flower, is a desert succulent—a plant that stores water in its stem to survive dry conditions. Its flowers smell like rotten meat to attract carrion flies and blowflies, which lay their eggs inside. The speckled petals add to the clever disguise. As the insects fly out, they help pollinate the stapelia.

# Stinking corpse lily

## *Rafflesia arnoldii*

Stinking corpse lily puts on quite a show in the wild. After sitting quietly on the forest floor for months, it blossoms with a loud hissing sound. It also gives off a terrible smell of rotting meat, drawing flies and beetles searching for dead flesh. As if that weren't enough, the flower produces heat to spread the stink. Its pollen is unusually thick, smelly, and sticky.

Its 40-in- (1-m-) wide flowers are the largest in the world!

Its flowers can grow up to 4-6 ft (1-2 m) in height.

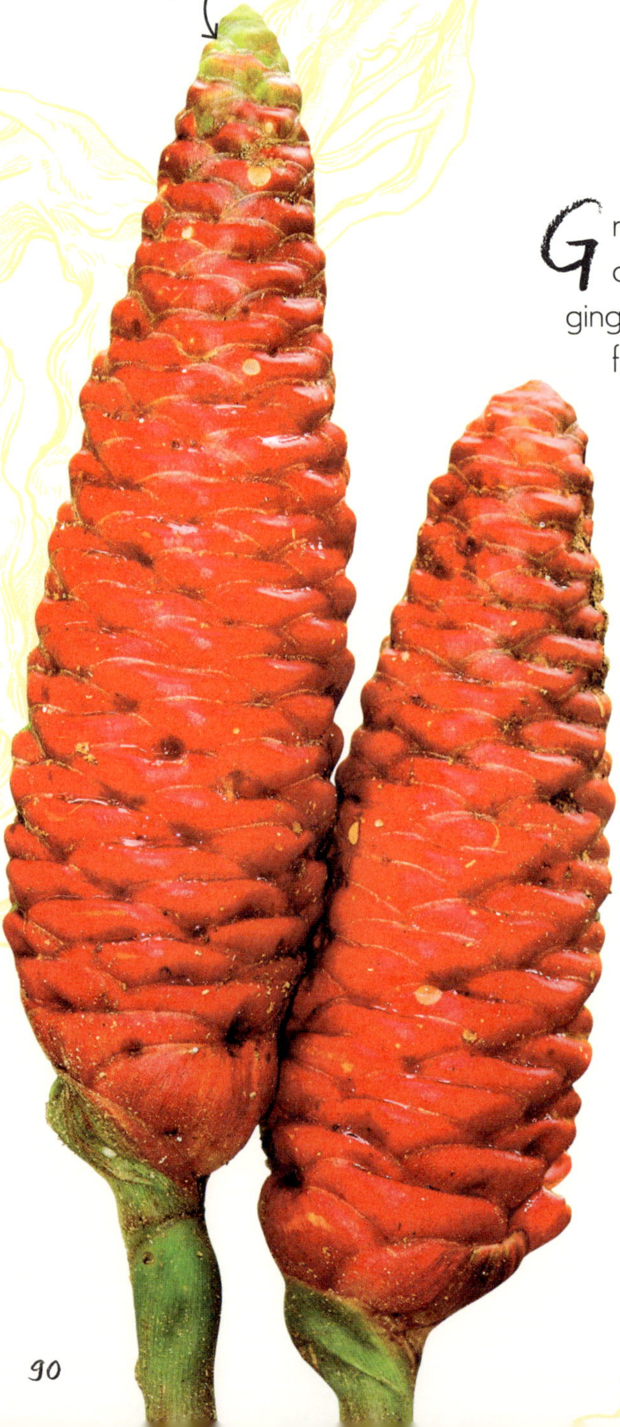

# Awapuhi

## Zingiber zerumbet

Growing tall by rivers and waterfalls, awapuhi is a sweet member of the ginger family. Its bright red, cone-shaped flowers are actually bracts. They begin as lime-green cones, from which tiny white flowers peek out. Once the plant has fully bloomed, the cones turn a dramatic red.

The juice inside the flowers is used to clean hair and make it shine. This is why some people also call this plant shampoo ginger.

Bell-shaped flowers with curled petals

Hyacinths grow from underground bulbs that store nutrients for the flowers.

# Hyacinth

## *Hyacinthus orientalis*

The vibrant blue hyacinths seem to come straight out of a mythical story. They were named after the Greek prince Hyacinthus, when they flowered at the same spot where he died. The starlike blossoms grow up a short spike, tucked between glossy leaves at the base. Their strong and fresh scent is a delight for bees, butterflies, and moths.

# Stinking arum

## *Amorphophallus titanum*

This clever plant has smelly flowers that stink like moldy cheese, rotting meat, or garlic. The awful smell can travel half a mile, tricking insects into coming close. As they search for food or a place to lay eggs, they help the flowers spread their pollen. Stinking arum flowers are the biggest inflorescences in the world—but they bloom for just one day.

*A frilly collar surrounds a thick central stalk that looks like a huge French baguette.*

Stinking arums can reach heights of more than 10 ft (3 m).

# Honeysuckle

## *Lonicera periclymenum*

Not all honeysuckle types are scented, but the ones that are have a lovely, sweet smell. Their long nectar tubes attract many insects and animals looking for a tasty treat. That's why honeysuckle is often called a "wildlife hotel." Its flowers are mainly pollinated by hawk moths, which use their long tongues to reach the nectar deep inside.

*Their flowers are a mix of white, pink, and yellow.*

## Why do flowers smell?

Smell is one of many ways that flowers can attract their pollinator mates. For those who can't see brightly colored flowers or who stop by a flower during nighttime when it's too dark, a scent can be a good signal. It allows them to find their favorite flowers from far away.

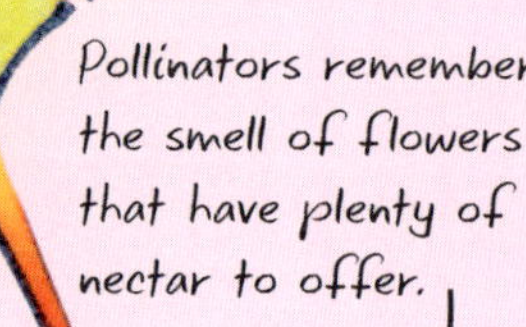

Pollinators remember the smell of flowers that have plenty of nectar to offer.

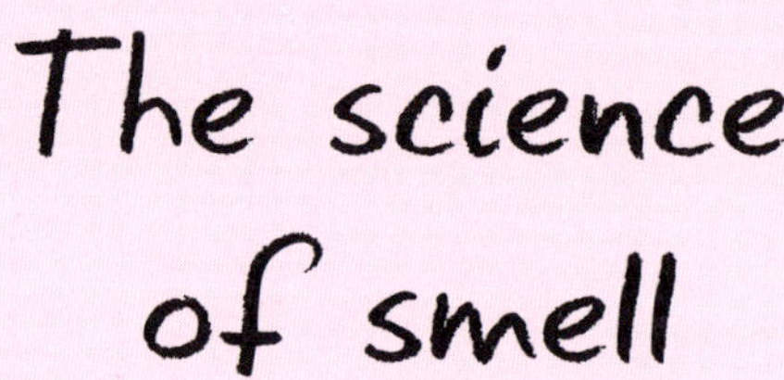

# The science of smell

Not all flowers produce smells that humans can recognize, but there are many flowers that do. Flowers make scents in their petals in cells called "scent factories." The cells contain natural chemicals that help flowers make and release all kinds of smells!

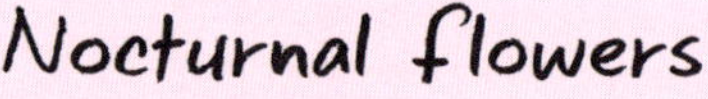

## Nocturnal flowers

While most flowers open in sunshine, some flowers save their show for moonlight. These are called nocturnal flowers. They lack bright colors, but their white petals glow in the dark. Nighttime pollinators, such as bats and moths, have poor eyesight. So, they follow strong scents of nocturnal flowers, like moonflowers, to find them.

## Making perfume

For centuries, some sweet-smelling flowers have been used to make scents. People extract the aroma of flowers in steam form and convert it into liquid essential oils. This process is called distillation. Today, there are many modern ways of perfume making.

Perfumers haven't been able to extract the smell of some flowers, called mute flowers, such as freesia.

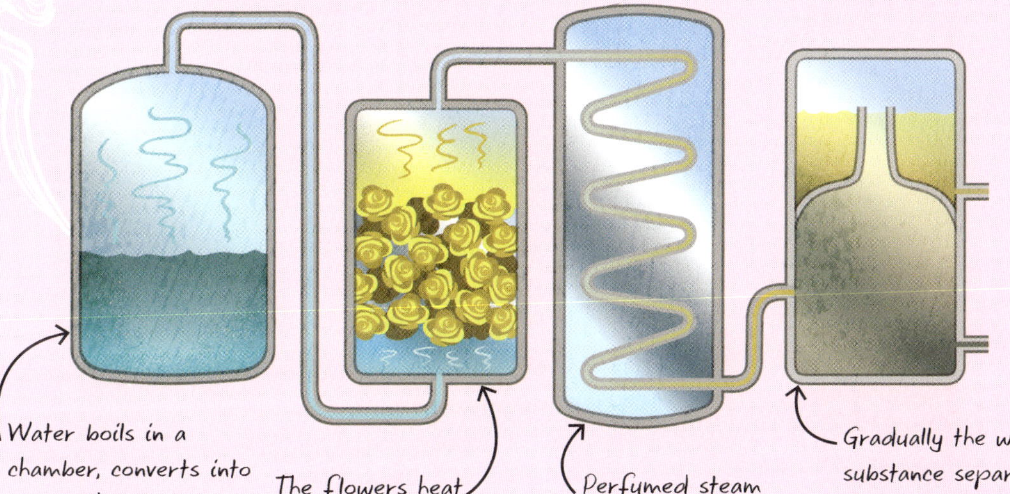


## Not always nice!

Not all flowers have a pleasant smell. Some flowers, like the stinking corpse lily, produce a horrible stench specially for their pollinators. They are known as "carrion flowers," and prefer to attract dung beetles, carrion flies, and other insects that scavenge for rotting meat.

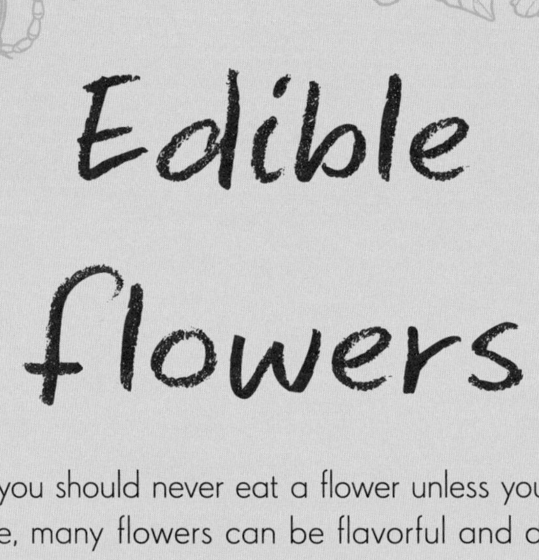


While you should never eat a flower unless you're sure it is safe, many flowers can be flavorful and delicious. For centuries, people have grown vegetables and edible flowers in their gardens to use in sweet and savory dishes. In fact, some vegetables, like broccoli, are actually flower buds. Edible flowers can be packed with nutrients and are used in all sorts of foods, from teas to desserts. Roses add flavour to treats, such as Turkish delight, and some candies like Parma Violets are named after the flowers they taste like!

# Violet

## *Viola odorata*

Many different types of violet are found around the world, but this species grows naturally in Europe and West Asia. Throughout Europe, violets are commonly used in cooking. In France, syrup of these flowers is added to many drinks, pastries, and desserts.

*The flowers can be blue, deep violet, or white.*

*Some people add violet flowers to salads for a pop of color and flavor.*

# Hibiscus

## *Hibiscus x rosa-sinensis*

Known for its attractive colors and big, trumpet-shaped blooms, the hibiscus is hard to miss. One of its most popular varieties is the Chinese hibiscus, or the China rose, often seen as a symbol of love. It is native to Africa, Central America, the Caribbean, and southern Asia. Some hibiscus flowers make aromatic tea and tasty juices. The flowers also lend their goodness to many medicines.

# Nigella

## *Nigella damascena*

The delicate, feathery, and green bracts of nigella surround their papery flowers, creating a soft, misty backdrop. This is why it's also called "love in a mist." Nigella is more commonly known for its seeds, which are used in foods. Some Muslims think the seeds can cure anything except death.

The strongly flavored seeds can be sprinkled on breads and cakes for a burst of flavor.

The flowers come in shades of blue, purple, or white.

# Mimosa

## *Acacia dealbata*

Vibrant popcorn-like mimosa flowers grow on giant trees known as "wattles" in mainland Australia and Tasmania. With their sweet, honeyed scent and zesty lemon flavor, they're a treat for the senses. The pollen-rich flowers can be cooked into delicious, sunshine-colored fritters. In Italy, these blooms are exchanged as part of the International Women's Day celebrations.

# Amaranth

## *Amaranthus sp.*

Most amaranth species are equally delightful in the garden and on the plate. While some of them are prized for their brightly colored leaves and striking flowers, others are grown for their high nutritional value. Only a handful of amaranth seeds can have the same amount of protein as a glass of milk!

Another species called love-lies-bleeding is adored for its crimson, trailing flowers.

This species of amaranth, called Joseph's coat, is popular for its tricolor leaves.

# Himalayan balsam

## *Impatiens glandulifera*

This beautiful flower thrives in the wilds of the Himalayas, blushing in shades of pink, purple, or white. This is why it's often called "kiss-me-on-the-mountain." Its blossoms are widely used in jams, jellies, salads, and drinks. Its name, *Impatiens*, means "impatient" because the seed pods burst open at the slightest touch!

# Magnolia

## *Magnolia grandiflora*

Among the earliest flowering plants, magnolia is the beetles' favorite. Known for its glossy green leaves and impressively large flowers, it is native to the southern US. The gingery-sweet flavored blooms are sometimes added to salads, desserts, and sushi across the US, the UK, and Southeast Asia.

Magnolia flowers can be as much as 12 in (30 cm) wide.

# Fennel

## *Foeniculum vulgare*

Although it thrives in moist conditions, fennel can survive in dry and sandy soil, and sometimes even droughts. All parts of this hardy plant are edible—adding a sweet and fresh flavor to savory dishes, sauces, and seasoning. Originally found in the Mediterranean region, fennel is now grown in many other parts of the world, too.

The bulbs of Florence fennel, a variety of fennel, make flavorful salads.

The yellow fennel flowers are shaped like tiny umbrellas.

# Pansy

## *Viola x wittrockiana*

The pansy is a hybrid child of the violet. This means it is made by cross-pollinating two different types of violet flower. While they resemble their parent flowers, they have bigger petals. Beautiful pansies are used as a garnish to make food look attractive.

# Cornflower

## *Centaurea cyanus*

The tough cornflower grows easily in poor soil and cold places but it needs plenty of sun. It doesn't belong to the corn family, but mostly pops up in cornfields. Although the "Blue Boy" is the most commonly found cornflower, its flowers also come in white, pink, and purple shades. Cornflowers have a mild peppery flavor and are mostly used as a garnish.

# Nasturtium

## *Tropaeolum majus*

This warm-weather flower may catch your eye as a twisted vine or low-growing bush. Its bright and peppery blossoms add a splash of color and flavor to many dishes, such as salads and stir-fries. In Europe and South American countries, including Peru, Brazil, and Chile, these delicious beauties are a much-loved treat.

*The leaves of the nasturtium plant look like mini parasols, or sun umbrellas.*

*The topmost petal extends into a long nectar spur, or tube, at the back.*

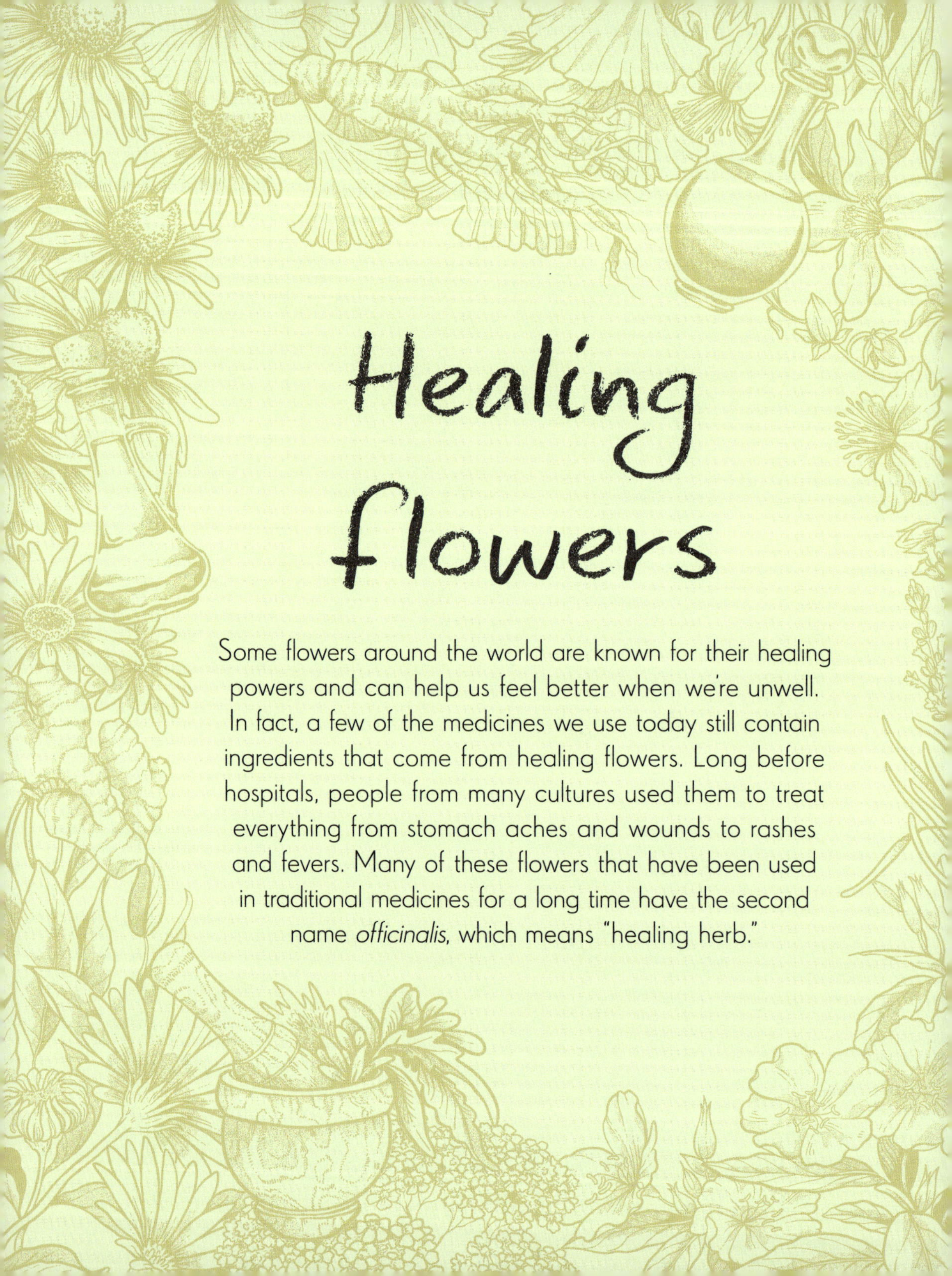

# Healing flowers

Some flowers around the world are known for their healing powers and can help us feel better when we're unwell. In fact, a few of the medicines we use today still contain ingredients that come from healing flowers. Long before hospitals, people from many cultures used them to treat everything from stomach aches and wounds to rashes and fevers. Many of these flowers that have been used in traditional medicines for a long time have the second name *officinalis*, which means "healing herb."

# Marigold

## *Calendula officinalis*

Marigolds belong to the daisy family, and are among the best-known healing flowers. Their vibrant colors and soft-scented leaves attract butterflies and bees. Ancient people used them to soothe and heal cuts and rashes. Today, they're added to moisturizers and lotions.

# Elderflower

## *Sambucus nigra*

Elderflowers are loved for their sweet flavor, but most of their parts are toxic until they're cooked well. People use both the berries and flowers to make all kinds of desserts and drinks, including wine. They're also packed with vitamin C, which helps boost our immune system so we don't get sick as easily.

Their white flowers grow in umbrellalike clusters.

*Although commonly called English lavender, the flower is not really native to England.*

# Lavender

## *Lavandula angustifolia*

Lavender helps people feel calm and relaxed. Its lovely, soothing smell makes it a go-to ingredient in soaps and oils. Lots of people use lavender to help them get a better night's sleep. Even bumblebees can't resist these purple beauties—they're among their absolute favorites!

# Chrysanthemum

## *Chrysanthemum x morifolium*

Chrysanthemums grow best in cool places, blooming every fall. Popular worldwide, they are especially prized during the Double Ninth Festival in China, where people sip chrysanthemum tea and enjoy their beauty in gardens and flower markets. For centuries, the flowers have been used in medicine because they're a good source of vitamins and help fight illnesses.

*The outer ring of petals is tightly packed and curls inward.*

*The flowers burst in many colors, including pink, purple, red, or orange.*

The flower heads grow up to 2 in (5 cm) wide.

# Butterfly pea

## *Clitoria ternatea*

This fast-growing summer vine scrambles its way up, curling on nearby plants or fences for support. Although a wildflower, the butterfly pea is a popular choice in gardens for its vibrant blue flowers. In Ayurveda, an ancient Indian medicine, the flowers are used to make calming teas.

# Coneflower

## *Echinacea purpurea*

Coneflowers are native to North America, where they have long been used in medicines for treating different ailments. The word *echinacea* comes from the Greek word for "sea urchin" because the flower's spiky center resembles the animal's spiny shell. The blossoms make lots of nectar, attracting a host of pollinators, including birds, butterflies, and bees.

Each floret in the dome-like center turns into a seed after pollination.

# St. John's wort

## *Hypericum perforatum*

Blooming in midsummer, around St. John's birthday, this flower is named after the biblical figure. It is widely used in medicines that help improve low moods. In ancient times, people believed that burning St. John's wort in huge bonfires warded off evil and brought prosperity.

# Evening primrose

## *Oenothera biennis*

True to its name, the evening primrose opens its flowers at sunset. Its fragrant, yellow blooms are adored by many nocturnal pollinators. The flowers are not just pretty, but are also rich in medicinal qualities. They're often used in treating skin problems.

*Evening primroses are also known as the "King's cure all" because of their many healing uses.*

Thin petals overlap to form a bowl-shaped flower.

# Yarrow

## *Achillea millefolium*

These tiny wild flowers grow in closely knit clusters in meadows. From ancient times, yarrows have been used to treat cuts and wounds. They also contain chemicals that can help fight infections. The flower's Latin name comes from the Greek hero Achilles, who used yarrow flowers to treat soldiers on the battlefield.

Huge clusters of these blooms grow very quickly.

# Ratchaphruek

## *Cassia fistula*

The golden yellow ratchaphruek flowers hang from branches, earning the tree the name "golden shower tree." They flourish in warm climates and grow in massive clusters. Ratchaphruek are the state flowers of Kerala, in India, and are known for their medicinal qualities. In ancient Indian medicine, they were called *aragvadha*, which means "disease killer."

Each flower has five petals and is 1 in (3.5 cm) wide.

Chamomile tea, made from dried chamomile flowers, is relished for its soothing effect.

# Chamomile

## *Matricaria chamomilla*

Chamomile, from the same family as sunflowers and daisies, is known for its sweet, delicate scent and flavor. These flowers are easy to grow and have been used for centuries to treat tummy and skin issues. Blooming from summer to fall, they bring beauty and healing wherever they grow.

These flowers look like daisies with white petals and a yellow center.

# Not quite flowers

Some plants produce flowers that turn into seeds, helping new plants grow nearby or far away. Others that don't bear flowers have clever ways of reproducing, or making new plants. Some fungi even make pretend flowers to fool pollinators into helping them spread.

## Cones

Some plants, like conifers, produce cones instead of flowers, which help them make seeds. Small, soft male cones are loaded with pollen that travels on the wind and gets trapped in the woody scales of large female cones. This is where seeds begin to form.

*The lichen is named after its red tops, which resemble the red coats once worn by British soldiers.*

## British soldier lichen

The bright red caps of British soldier lichen stand out on tall green stalks. These aren't flowers but spore-producing parts. Spores are tiny cells that can develop into new plants. However, the British soldier lichen doesn't really grow through these spores. It reproduces when small bits of lichen fall off and grow nearby.

## Rock cress fungus

A fungus called *Puccinia monoica* stops the rock cress plant from growing real flowers. Instead, it makes bright yellow, flowerlike structures, which are covered in sticky spores that look like nectar. Pollinators are tricked into landing on them. As they fly away, the spores stick to their feet and spread to other plants.

As spores are carried to other grasses, the fungus spreads and makes more pretend flowers.

## Fungus flower

Another fungus called *Fusarium xyrophilum* tricks bees by mimicking a flower. It grows a fake bloom on top of the yellow-eyed grass bud, matching the real flower's color and scent. Bees visit it in search of pollen, but instead pick up the fungus's spores.

## Bracts

Plants that grow bracts have a good reason for it. Bracts act like false petals, helping to attract animal visitors. For instance, bougainvillea has tiny flowers, so it grows large colorful bracts that look like petals. These bright, leaflike parts catch the attention of pollinators and guide them to the small flowers hidden inside.

# Conservation

An ecosystem is where living things, such as plants and animals, and nonliving things like rocks, sunlight, and water coexist. It can be as large as our planet or as small as a pond. Each member plays a vital role in keeping the balance. Flowers are important because they offer food and homes to many creatures. Without them, the ecosystem might collapse.

*Trees and plants are cut down to make roads.*

## Habitat destruction

Forests are essential because they host a variety of flowers, plants, and animals. But people are cutting them down to build more houses, buildings, and roads. As a result, many animals and plants are struggling to survive, and some may disappear forever.

## How can we help?

There are lots of ways to help nature. Here are some simple things you can do to protect flowers and the wildlife they support. Every small action can make a big difference.

**Do not pick wildflowers**
If you see flowers in the wild, take time to appreciate their beauty. Smell them and observe the insects they attract, but leave the blooms where they are so they can grow and make seeds.

**Grow a garden**
Planting flowers in your garden is a great way to care for the environment. It creates little ecosystems where animals, insects, and plants can all live together. More gardens and green spaces mean more homes for all kinds of wildlife.

**Protect and rebuild ecosystems**
It's important that we do everything we can to protect our ecosystems for the future of our planet. Around the world, many programs are helping countries bring back lost habitats, replant native flowers, and support wildlife.

# Glossary

**annual plant**
Plant that grows, produces flowers and seeds, and dies all within one year

**anther**
Part of a flower, at the end of the stamen, which produces and contains pollen (*see pollen*)

**biennial plant**
Plant that lives for two years. It grows stems and leaves in the first year, and flowers and seeds in the second

**bract**
Leaflike structure found at the base of a flower, often resembling a petal

**bulb**
Fat, fleshy stem of some plants that is buried underground and acts as a food store

**carrion**
Decaying flesh of a dead animal

**conifer**
Refers to group of cone-bearing evergreen trees with needlelike leaves

**cross-pollination**
Transfer of pollen from the male part of one flower to the female part of another flower

**disk floret**
Tiny tubular flowers clustered in the center of a flower head of some plants, such as daisies

**distillation**
Process of extracting the pure part of something. This is usually done by heating the substance in a liquid to make steam, which is then cooled back into liquid to collect its essence

**double flower**
Flower with multiple layers of petals, making it look full and big

**ecosystem**
Community of living organisms that interact with each other and their surroundings

**filament**
Long, thin stalk that holds up the anther

**floret**
Small flower that's part of a large flower

**flower head**
Cluster of many small flowers grouped together so they look like a single big flower

**fungus**
Group of organisms that feed on decayed matter like dead leaves. Separate from the plants, they include molds and mushrooms

**germination**
Process in which a seed begins to sprout and grow into a young plant, or seedling

**hybrid**
Offspring, or young, produced by two different plant species

**inflorescence**
Cluster of flowers arranged on a plant's stem

**legume**
Plant within the pea family that has its seeds in pods, such as beans, lentils, and peas

**lichen**
Organism formed by a partnership between an alga and a fungus that share a body

**nectar**
Sugary fluid produced by special glands in flowers to attract pollinating animals

**nectar spur**
Tubular structure of a flower, usually extending from petals or sepals, that stores nectar

**nocturnal**
Awake and active at night

**ovary**
Egg-producing female reproductive part in a flower

**perennial plant**
Plant that survives for more than two years

**petal**
Part of a flower that is often colorful and attracts pollinators

**pigment**
Chemical that gives something its color

**pollen**
Powdery substance made by a flower that helps the plant reproduce (*see reproduction*)

**pollination**
Transfer of pollen from the male part of the flower to the female part, causing new seeds or fruit to grow

**pollinator**
Something that transfers pollen from the male part of a flower to the female part

**ray floret**
Strap-shaped flower that forms the outer ring of a flower head

**reproduction**
Production of offspring

**seedpod**
Protective casing containing the seeds of a plant

**self-pollination**
Transfer of pollen from the male part of one flower to the female part of the same flower

**sepal**
Small, leaflike part at the base of a flower that protects its buds or petals

**sp.**
Short for "species;" refers to all species within a genus

**species**
Distinct group of animals or plants that share similar features

**spore**
Dustlike particle, similar to a seed, used by fungi, ferns, and mosses to spread and grow new plants

**stamen**
Male reproductive part of a flower that includes the filament and anther

**stigma**
Tip of the female part of a flower that receives pollen

**toxin**
Poisonous substance

**tuber**
Thickened, swollen part of an underground stem or root that can store food for plants

**var.**
Short for "variety;" a natural variation between two of the same flowers

**wetland**
Very wet areas of land, such as marshes, bogs, and swamps

**wilt**
When a plant or flower becomes weak and droops because it lacks water or is dying

# Index

**Senior Editor** Radhika Haswani
**Editor** Syed Tuba Javed
**Senior US Editor** Megan Douglass
**Art Editor** Nishtha Gupta
**Assistant Art Editor** Tanya Varkey P
**Pre-production Designer** Bimlesh Tiwary
**Pre-production Image Coordinator** Neeraj Bhatia
**Senior Picture Researcher** Aditya Katyal
**Senior Jackets Art Editor** Dheeraj Arora
**Managing Editor** Roohi Sehgal
**Managing Art Editors** Diane Peyton Jones, Ivy Sengupta
**Associate Publisher** Gemma Farr
**Production Editor** Vishal Bhatia
**Production Controller** Tony Blain
**India Creative Head** Malavika Talukder
**Art Director** Mabel Chan

**Consultant** Douglas Palmer

## About the author:

Maddie Bailey is a young horticulturist and writer based in London. With her expertise in the subject, she has authored many amazing titles, including *The Hidden Histories of Flowers* and *The Hidden Histories of Houseplants.*

## DK would like to thank:

Roohi Rais, Mohd Zishan, and Mitravinda V K for design support; Ridhima Sikka, Rituraj Singh, and Manpreet Kaur for picture research assistance; Jonathan Melmoth for proofreading; Helen Peters for the index.

## From the author:

A special thank you to those who supported me during the making of this book—especially Cris and Cheo at Alma Verde. I hope those who read this book will enjoy reading it as much as I enjoyed writing it.

The publisher would like to thank the following for their kind permission to reproduce their photographs: (Key: a-above; b-below/bottom; c-center; f-far; l-left; r-right; t-top)

**2 Alamy Stock Photo:** Image Source Limited / Craig Tuttle / Travel RM. **3 Alamy Stock Photo:** Picture Partners. **5 Adobe Stock:** Paul (br). **6 Alamy Stock Photo:** imageBROKER.com / jspix (bl). **Dreamstime.com:** Scphoto48 (br); Verastuchelova (cl); Troichenko (bc). **7 Getty Images / iStock:** Anna Bryukhanova (br). **9 Adobe Stock:** kostiuchenko (bc). **Dreamstime.com:** Mykola Ohorodnyk (cra); Vilor (br). **11 Dreamstime.com:** Flynt (tl). **13 Dreamstime.com:** Julija Petrovskaja (r). **14 Dreamstime.com**: Tamara Kulikova (l). **15 Getty Images / iStock:** Maria Forbes (b). **16 Alamy Stock Photo:** John Anderson (l). **17 Dreamstime.com:** Ksushsh (r). **18 Adobe Stock:** Unclesam (l). **19 Getty Images / iStock:** Oksana Lyskova (r). **20 Depositphotos Inc:** Zetor2010 (b). **21 Getty Images / iStock:** ksena32 (r). **22 Getty Images / iStock:** scisettialfio (t). **23 Adobe Stock:** Sarit Richerson (b). **24 Adobe Stock:** Shy Radar (b). **25 Dreamstime.com:** Sgoodwin4813 (r). **27 Alamy Stock Photo:** Yon Marsh Science (bl). **Dreamstime.com:** Ondrej Prosicky (tl). **Getty Images / iStock:** Calvin Jennings (cr). **29 Dreamstime.com:** Pran Yadee (b). **30 Dreamstime.com:** Akarawut Lohacharoenvanich (l). **31 Alamy Stock Photo:** Nature Picture Library / Paul Harcourt Davies (b). **32 Photo by Ron Parsons:** (l). **33 Getty Images / iStock:** Alfribeiro. **34 Alamy Stock Photo:** Electra Kay-Smith (b). **35 Adobe Stock:** LianeM (b). **36 Dreamstime.com:** Bos11 (bl). **37 Adobe Stock:** nazuna art (tr). **39 Alamy Stock Photo:** Robert Wyatt (b). **40 Adobe Stock:** Renán Vicencio Uribe (tl). **41 Alamy Stock Photo:** imageBROKER.com / Christian Hütter (r). **42 Getty Images:** Stockbyte / Ed Reschke (tl). **43 Alamy Stock Photo:** José María Barres Manuel (r). **45 Getty Images / iStock:** Oleg Charykov (b). **46 Alamy Stock Photo:** Gerry Bishop (l). **47 Alamy Stock Photo:** Botany vision (r). **48 Alamy Stock Photo:** Manfred Ruckszio (l). **49 Dreamstime.com:** Karin De Mamiel (b). **51 Adobe Stock:** Aquiya (b). **52 Alamy Stock Photo:** piemags / nature (b). **53 Science Photo Library:** Bob Gibbons (t). **54 Dreamstime.com:** Joanne Harris (l).

First American Edition, 2026
Published in the United States by DK Publishing,
a division of Penguin Random House LLC
1745 Broadway, 20th Floor, New York, NY 10019


26 27 28 29 30 10 9 8 7 6 5 4 3 2 1
001–345734–Feb/2026



Published in Great Britain by Dorling Kindersley Limited

ISBN: 979-8-2171-3395-6



Printed and bound in China

**www.dk.com**

This book was made with Forest Stewardship Council™ certified paper—one small step in DK's commitment to a sustainable future.
Learn more at **www.dk.com/uk/information/sustainability**

**55 Dreamstime.com:** Horst Lieber (b). **56 Alamy Stock Photo:** Nature Picture Library / MYN / Lily Kumpe (l). **58 Alamy Stock Photo:** Nature Picture Library / Chris Mattison (bl). **59 Getty Images:** Moment / Robbie Goodall (tr). **61 GAP Photos:** Nova Photo Graphik (r). **62 Alamy Stock Photo:** Nigel Cattlin (bl). **63 Alamy Stock Photo:** Asist RF Arkiv. **64 Alamy Stock Photo:** Konrad Wothe / Minden Pictures (b). **65 Dreamstime.com:** Ksena2009. **66 Dreamstime.com:** Picture Partners (b). **67 Alamy Stock Photo:** Arterra Picture Library / Clement Philippe. **68 Adobe Stock:** Daniel Schoenen / imageBROKER. **69 Getty Images / iStock:** marcophotos. **70 Alamy Stock Photo:** Derek Harris (b). **71 Dreamstime.com:** Alfio Scisetti (tr). **72 Alamy Stock Photo:** imageBROKER / S Charlie Brown (b). **Dreamstime.com:** David Havel (tl). **73 Adobe Stock:** Paul (bl). **Alamy Stock Photo:** Andy Sands / naturepl.com (tl). **Getty Images / iStock:** 153photostudio (cr). **75 Alamy Stock Photo:** Robert Garrigus. **76 Shutterstock.com:** Quang Ho (l). **77 Dreamstime.com:** Picture Partners (r). **78 Dreamstime.com:** Karen Burgess (bl). **79 Adobe Stock:** Sarawut (r). **80 Shutterstock.com:** Manfred Ruckszio (l). **81 Adobe Stock:** Brian Woolman (r). **83 Alamy Stock Photo:** Mike P Shepherd (b). **84 Depositphotos Inc:** jimbo3904 (l). **85 Adobe Stock:** H.A.Colijn (r). **86 Adobe Stock:** sathit (l). **87 Getty Images:** Corbis / Paul Starosta (tr). **88 Alamy Stock Photo:** imageBROKER / Erich Geduldig (tl). **89 Dreamstime.com:** Maizal Maizal (br). **90 Depositphotos Inc:** Tanagron (bl). **91 Dreamstime.com:** Steve Lagreca (tr). **92 Adobe Stock:** Maizal (l). **93 Adobe Stock:** Garden Guru (b). **94 Alamy Stock Photo:** Panoramic Images (tr). **Dreamstime.com:** Linda Lombardo (bl). **95 Dreamstime.com:** Svitlana Yefimkina (tr). **Getty Images / iStock:** asavliuk (br). **97 Alamy Stock Photo:** lophius (br). **98 Alamy Stock Photo:** Nature Picture Library / Martin Gabriel (l). **99 Dreamstime.com:** Sarah2 (r). **100 Dreamstime.com:** NetPix (r). **101 Dreamstime.com:** Wirestock (b). **102 Dreamstime.com:** Nadin333 (l). **103 Dreamstime.com:** Helga11 (b). **104 Getty Images / iStock:** emer1940 (b). **105 GAP Photos:** (r). **106 Alamy Stock Photo:** Susie McCaffrey (l). **107 Dreamstime.com:** Valery Prokhozhy (b). **109 Dreamstime.com:** Aleksandr Volkov (b). **110 Dreamstime.com:** Melica (b). **111 GAP Photos:** Dave Zubraski (r). **112 Dreamstime.com:** Sanjiv Shukla (b). **113 Dreamstime.com:** Noppharat (tr). **114 Dreamstime.com:** Alfio Scisetti (b). **115 Dreamstime.com:** Antonel. **116 Dreamstime.com:** Photographieundmehr (bl). **117 Dreamstime.com:** Voltan1 (r). **118 Dreamstime.com:** Appfind (t). **119 Dreamstime.com:** Antonel (r). **120 Getty Images:** Stone / Ed Reschke (bl). **121 Glen Lee, Regina, SK, Canada:** (cl). **Dreamstime.com:** Margojh (br). Lauren A. Ré: (tr). **122 Alamy Stock Photo:** Sue Cunningham Photographic (b). **Dreamstime.com:** Wirestock (cl). **123 Adobe Stock:** Anastasia Amraeva (cl). **Getty Images / iStock:** E+ / SolStock (tr, br). **125 Dreamstime.com:** Aleksandr Volkov (br)

**Cover images:** *Front:* **Alamy Stock Photo:** Picture Partners bc; *Back:* **Alamy Stock Photo:** imageBROKER / Erich Geduldig cla; **Dreamstime.com:** Margojh cra; **Science Photo Library:** Paul Whitehill ca; *Spine:* **Alamy Stock Photo:** Picture Partners cb